If I Were an Alligator

By Meg Gaertner

level 2 little blue readers

www.littlebluehousebooks.com

Little Blue House is distributed by North Star Editions:
sales@northstareditions.com | 888-417-0195

Produced for Little Blue House by Red Line Editorial.

Photographs ©: Shutterstock Images, cover, 13 (top), 23 (top), 23 (bottom); iStockphoto, 4, 7, 9, 10–11, 13 (bottom), 14, 17 (top), 17 (bottom), 18, 24 (top left), 24 (top right), 24 (bottom left), 24 (bottom right); John Serrao/Science Source, 21

Library of Congress Control Number: 2020913855

ISBN
978-1-64619-309-7 (hardcover)
978-1-64619-327-1 (paperback)
978-1-64619-363-9 (ebook pdf)
978-1-64619-345-5 (hosted ebook)

Printed in the United States of America
Mankato, MN
012021

About the Author

Meg Gaertner enjoys reading, writing, dancing, and being outside. She recently learned how to tell alligators and crocodiles apart. She lives in Minnesota.

Table of Contents

If I Were an Alligator **5**

Food and Safety **15**

Other Behaviors **19**

Glossary **24**

Index **24**

If I Were an Alligator

I would live in fresh water.

I would swim in slow-moving rivers.

I would have a strong, spiky tail.
It would push me along as I swam.

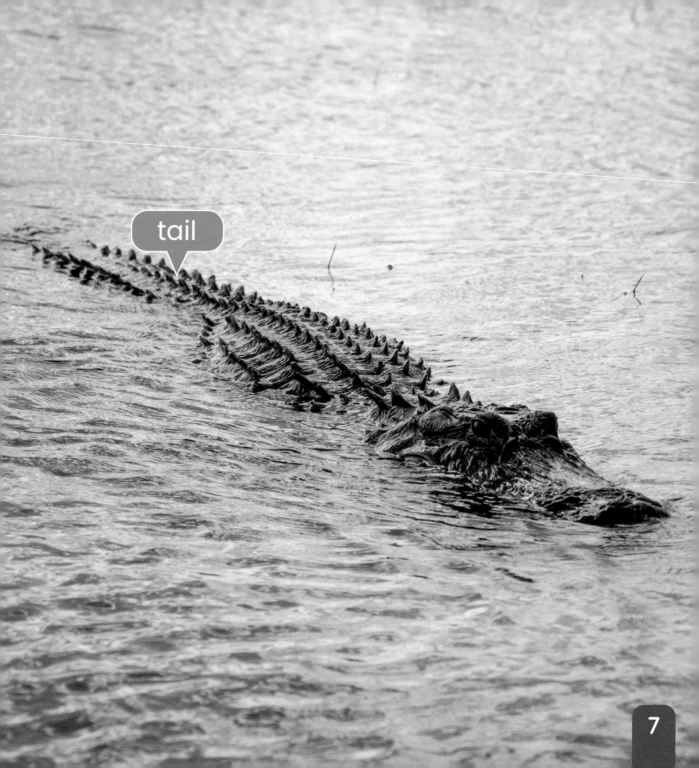

I would have webbing between my toes. My webbed feet would help me swim.

I would have four
short legs.
I would not be able to
move quickly on land.

I would have a wide snout and two nostrils.
I would be able to breathe even if most of my body was underwater.

Food and Safety

I would have hard skin and sharp teeth.

My skin and teeth would keep me safe.

I would have a
strong bite.

I would break open the
shells of turtles.

I would also eat fish and
small animals.

Other Behaviors

I would sit in the sunlight.

I would let the sun warm my body.

I would make a hole
in the mud.
I would stay in the hole
during cold weather.
The mud would keep
me warm.

I would lay eggs in a nest on the ground.
My babies would be very small at first.
But they would grow much bigger over time.

Glossary

nostrils

teeth

tail

webbing

Index

B
bite, 16

E
eggs, 22

N
nest, 22

S
snout, 12

24